Aim Pure, Putt Pure

AIMPUREPUTTPURE

A complete guide to putting:

Green Reading fundamentals
The ideal pre-putt routine
The Quiet Eye technique to stay in the zone
Eye exercises
Putting Drills

You may have picked up this book because you are struggling with your putting, or you might just want to confirm that you are doing everything visually possible to putt your best!

As an optometrist I have a deep understanding of the impact of vision on aiming sports particularly putting. I have helped my patients and clients to maximise their vision with exercises and corrections for over 20 years.

Now I am going to help you too……..

Contents

Section 3 Eye Exercises

Section 4: Strategy/How to aim

Section 5: Drills for skills

Section 6 : Miscellaneous

Glossary of terms

Summary

Introduction

'If we keep doing what we are doing we are going to keep getting what we have been getting' Stephen R Covey

To explain putting to players of all levels,
with an emphasis on optimising your vision for the task.

That is the aim of this book.

Clear and concise.

How often have you played with a fellow golfer who hits the ball poorly, has an average pitching and chipping game, but still matches your score?

To hit the ball long and straight consistently you do need certain physical attributes.

But anyone can be a great putter.

It's an area of the game which will give you big returns if you invest time on improving it. I also believe it will maximise your enjoyment of the game.

Why do people struggle with putting?
Usually they don't have a clear plan in mind
They have a vague (or even an incorrect) target
They have poor distance control

And since line and length have to match up, if one or both are incorrect they will miss.

Sometimes they will get one right (line or length) and have a 'good day'.

Not knowing your weakness will lead to a lack of confidence.

The aim of this book is to give you the tools to :

1) Clearly explain how and why you can be an amazing putter
2) Give you confidence to rely on your putting with structured practice
3) Be a resource for you to refer back to and fix your own putting if bad habits creep back in.

1.What is visually important for golfers?

Acuity:

Having a clear image is important in seeing subtle breaks in the green and visualising your target accurately.

Opticians measure the level of clarity you can achieve as 'visual acuity'.

If you can see 20/20 (known as 6/6 in the UK) you have a good level of vision. If you cannot you may need help to get to that level of vision.

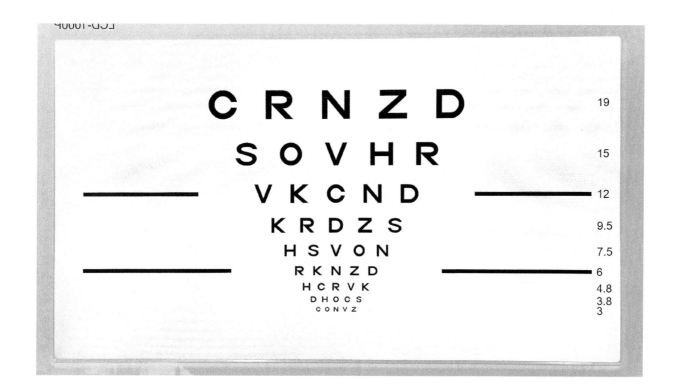

See your Optometrist/Eye Doctor to establish if you need a correction (glasses/contacts/laser), to give you the clearest view.

Astigmatism is a type of prescription which is relatively common. Astigmatism causes round objects to look elongated. It is caused by a non spherical eye. It results in a direction specific prescription. Some people mask astigmatism by squeezing the eyes temporarily, which gives temporary clarity. Doing this for longer periods of time may fatigue the eyes resulting in inconsistent visual performance. It might also cause headaches.

Peripheral vision:
by taking more information from your 'side vision' you can have a better perception of the overall slope of the green (important for longer putts).

Depth perception: This is important for distance control (speed and distance)

Visualisation: building a picture in your mind to see and plan the putt. You can practise this.

2. Depth perception (3D vision) and putting

In a normally functioning visual system the two eyes point at an object from two slightly different angles creating overlapping images.

The brain adapts these two single images into one 3D image. That's how we get depth perception.

If the eyes don't point close enough together, then the two images can get close to separating which can stress the visual system causing tiredness (i.e your eye muscles are working too hard to stop you getting a double image)

If you get a double image the brain might learn to ignore the second image. This is called suppression (like closing your eye without actually closing it).

If suppression happens for too long at a young age (during the critical period of visual development) it leads to deep suppression known as amblyopia (lazy eye). That is why it's important for children to have regular eye tests before the age of 8 to fix these problems.

If we don't have good depth perception we will struggle to judge the length of a putt as well. Sometimes players judge long putts well at the beginning of a round but at the end of a round (or rounds) their visual system fatigues and they struggle.

This is where eye muscle exercises can be beneficial.

3. The Setup

3a. Eye Dominance

Which eye is my dominant eye?
Does it matter?

Your dominant eye processes information faster than your non dominant eye
You should use your dominant eye to read putts and line putts up.

If you hold your hands up in front of you, overlapping.

There should be a small gap between the two hands
Aim at and centre a distant target in the gap
Now close one eye only and open it again
Now close the other eye only and open it again
When you closed your dominant eye the target disappeared

Now you know which is your dominant eye .

If you are unsure an Optician can confirm this with another method for checking distance dominance. This is known as the fogging method for eye dominance.

When you take your putting stance, ideally, if you dropped a ball from near your dominant eye it would hit the ball on the ground that you would be putting. i.e **Your dominant eye should be directly above the ball (or just inside) when you address your putt.**

This would help ensure you are looking squarely down the line of your putt to help avoid a parallax error.

What is parallax:

Parallax refers to the change in the apparent position of an object when viewed from different points.

The image below demonstrates parallax. Viewing directly above the golf ball to measure its size on a ruler. If we are directly above the ball we see the correct size. If we view the ball from an angle i.e slightly to either side we would get the wrong reading.

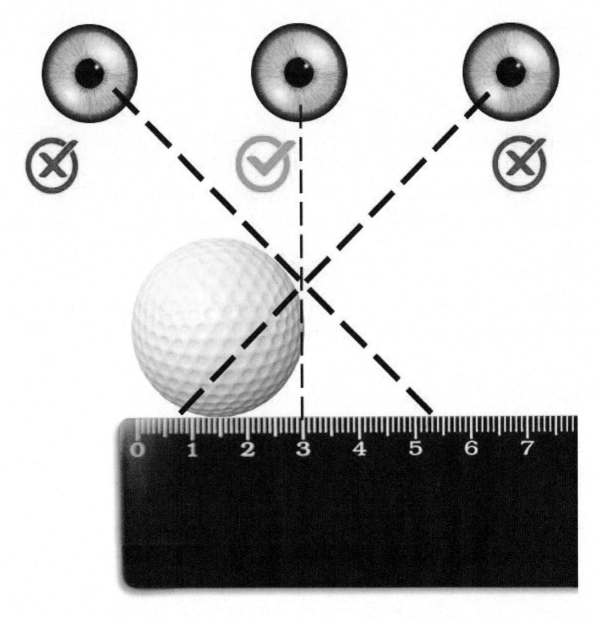

Relating this back to putting, we need to be lined up from our dominant eye to look directly down the line of the putt. If not, we see the putt to the left or the right of the actual line.

3b. Ball Position

How close should I stand to the ball?

Imagine a line between your ball and the hole
At address if you are too far over the ball you will be aiming to the left of the hole.

If you are not close enough to the ball you will be aiming to the right of the hole

If you are directly over the ball you will be square to the target and aiming correctly down the line. This is essential in avoiding a parallax error.

You can also use a putting mirror to make sure your eye position is optimal in relation to the ball.

The correct position may also be optimised by having the correct length of putter. Get a fitting, or see an expert club fitter for a modification.

3c. The basics of alignment and parallax

If your eyes are over the ball you are looking directly down the target line to the point you are aiming at (ball to target line)
Your body (feet, shoulders and hips) are not directly over the ball. Your eyes are.
If your body aims at the target as well your body will be closed to the target. The two lines will converge.
Your body actually needs to aim on a parallel target line. So if you are right handed your body will be aiming to the left of your ball line.
We call this ideal set up 'square'
Imagine a set of train tracks pointing towards the target. Your body will line up with one side of the track. Your putter face will line up with the other side of the track.
Both sides of the track will point towards the target but from a fractionally different point. The train track doesn't become narrow on its way to the target.

Square alignment:

Open (shoulders and hips aiming left) vs Closed (shoulders and hips aiming right)

Tip: If you know your feet are square to the target then you can use an imaginary line from back foot to front foot as a reference line and putt parallel to this. Straight back straight through.

3d. Intermediate target alignment

It is easier to line up to a target close to you than to the hole. This is known as a spot target. Once you read your putt and visualise the path the ball is going to take, find a spot on the ground a few feet away from you along that path. Line your feet up square to that imaginary target, line your putter face up to that imaginary target.

Visualisation is the ability to form a mental picture in your mind. If we draw a line extending from the spot target this is known as the **aim point**.

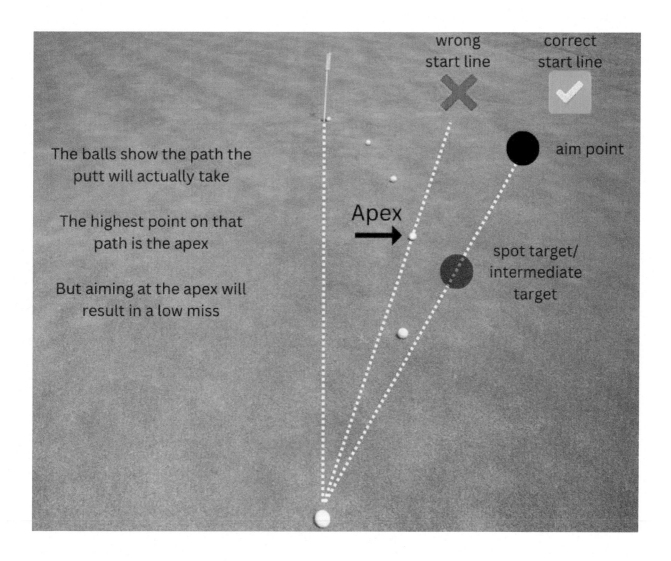

3e. How to use a putting mirror to check your set up

Putting mirrors will give you feedback on eye position, shoulder position and face alignment of the putter at address.

When you have assumed the putting position with the mirror in place, your dominant eye should be directly over the ball (or just inside). That's where there is a gap in the mirror for the ball, so ***you shouldn't see your eye***. If you can see your eye at the bottom section of the mirror, you are too far away. If you can see your eye at the top section of the mirror you are too close.

Your shoulders should be square to the target. The putter face should be square to the target .

Tilting the mirror up at an angle can help you to make sure your shoulder motion is correct during the stroke. The aim is to have minimum body movement from a tilt and sway perspective. Set up square stay square. Minimise the variables.

Eyes too far back
from ball

4. Should I get a putter fitting?

100% yes!!! And the earlier the better, otherwise you may ingrain some compensations around an incorrect putter, which will take time to get rid of.

Or you could just guess or "choose by feel" (please don't do this!!)

For some players half the strokes on the card come from their putter, so you want to choose your putter with assistance.

-Make sure the lie angle is correct (the putter should lie flat to the green) otherwise the heel or toe could snag the ground slightly causing the head to twist.

-Make sure the length is correct

This will help for posture/comfort

It will also help you to naturally be directly over the ball which is crucial for alignment.

Make sure the loft (and dynamic loft) is optimised for the greens you play regularly.

How much loft should a putter have ?

static loft 3 degrees   dynamic loft -1 degree

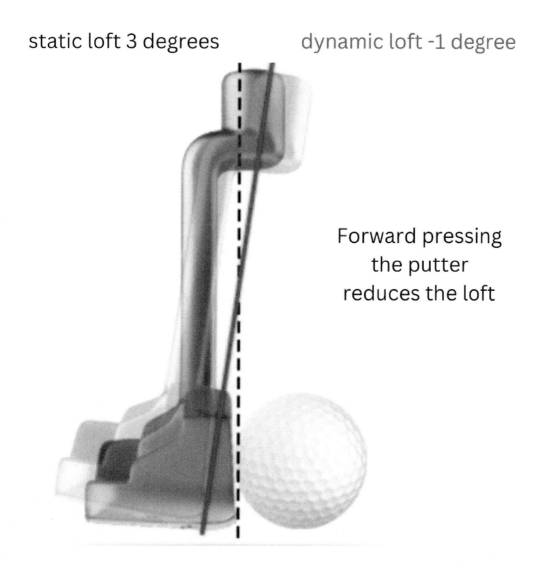

Forward pressing
the putter
reduces the loft

Loft is needed on a putter because as the ball rests on the green it pushes down slightly into the grass. The loft is therefore needed to lift the ball up and onto the surface for an end-over-end smooth roll.

If you have too little loft on your putter it will drive the ball into the green making it difficult to get it rolling quickly. Too much loft and ball will hop on impact and skid more before rolling out.

The optimum putter loft is 3-3.5 degrees.
The loft that comes set on the putter is called 'static loft'.
Nearly all golfers either add or take away loft at impact due to their stroke tendencies – this is known as dynamic loft.
A lot of players de-loft as a "trigger" in the putt routine (eg Jordan Spieth, Phil Mickelson)

Having the correct amount of loft allows you to produce the correct launch angle.
Some loft is needed for slow greens to get the ball in the air initially and then rolling. If the loft is too high, it causes the ball to skid.
Less loft is needed for faster/true greens.
Delofting a putter could cause the ball to travel further.
The sooner the ball gets back on the ground the more predictable its roll/path is.
The best putters get the ball rolling sooner.

Tip - When putting from the fringe don't deloft your putter as you want the ball to get up first to clear the fringe.

5. Aim small to miss small

Always aim precisely to make your misses closer.
I was once told that for long lag putts the aim was to get it within a 3 foot circle. There is a difference between what you aim for and how you manage your expectations. The hole is always the target. If you aim for a three foot circle, you will be outside that sometimes. If you aim for the hole it might not always go in but you will accept it being within the three foot circle.

Always aim precisely to make your misses closer

I divide the hole into smaller sections, be as specific as possible outside left edge, left edge, inside left edge, 1/3 in from left, left of centre, straight, right of centre, 1/3 in from right, inside right edge, right edge, outside right edge.

There are variations of this. A friend of mine visualises where he wants the ball to enter the hole like on a clock face.
Whatever works for you, but the point is to be precise and aim small to miss small.

6. The mental side of putting

a) Commiting to your line/Avoiding mental chatter

How many times have you been over a putt and had second thoughts before the putt. "It can't break that much" or "I need to allow more break".

You have already picked your line and set up to that. But the doubt over the ball will often result in you missing the putt

The subconscious mind is powerful. The doubt may cause you to open/shut the putter face at the last second, or you might attempt to steer the putt with your new last second line in mind.

This will result in a poor stroke which probably will not end well.

Commit to your line, put the best stroke you can on it. Before you putt, have ZERO thoughts. Mental chatter prior to a swing or a putt is a recipe for doubt and disaster. If it doesn't go in, that is ok. But if doubt kills your stroke you will dwell on it and it might affect your next shot(s).

A good example of this is putting through your own shadow.

In your mind you have a clear picture of how the putt is going to roll, from the moment it hits your putter face to when it drops in the hole. You see this as an imaginary line, like Puttview or a shot tracer. When you are committed you put a good stroke on it, it rolls end over end and traces the line.

A shadow doesn't bump your ball off line. Read that again. Of course it can't.

But it can interrupt you **seeing** that imaginary line as you stand over the ball. It can give you doubt and interrupt your "*flow*". You can't see your imaginary line any more.
The solution for this is to step back if you have doubt, recheck your line, breath, commit to a good stroke on your intended line

and then most importantly don't look up as you make your putt. Listen as the ball hits the hole.

Remember doubt is the killer and ruins momentum so if you have thoughts when you are over the ball, reset. Don't blag your way through it.

What is a downhill slider?

It's a fast downhill putt that breaks left to right.

For a left to right putt if you look up at impact the putter face stays slightly open causing you to miss on the low side.
The more anxious you get about a slider the more you might look up and it "slides" away from you.
The fix is to be extra careful about staying in your posture and not looking up early.
Listen to the ball going in and trust your start line and aim point.

b) Managing expectations

Sometimes I miss a putt but I make it! What do I mean?

You can do everything right, set up, stroke, perfect pace, perfect line, and the ball still might not go in. But in my head that's a putt I made. Because I can only control what I can control. So if it hits a spike mark or the wind gusts or the hole is crowned, well, things happen. If I do my bit, I'm gonna move on pretty swiftly.

One putt doesn't define if you are or are not a 'good putter'. Your statistics over time and your results do.

c) What is strokes gained putting

"Strokes gained recognizes that sinking a 20-foot putt represents a better performance than sinking a three-foot putt, even though they both count as a single stroke on the scorecard. Strokes gained assigns a number to this intuition. Though strokes gained has roots in some fancy mathematics developed at the dawn of the computer age, there is an elegant simplicity to a stat that, at its core, merely involves subtracting two numbers." - Mark Broadie, Columbia Business School, developer of Strokes Gained, and author of Every Shot Counts.

From 7 feet, 10 inches the average number of putts to hole out is 1.5. If a player one-putts from that distance, he gains 0.5 strokes. If he two-putts, he loses 0.5 strokes. If he three-putts, he loses 1.5 strokes:

Strokes Gained - Putting

2010 Baseline Probabilities

DISTANCE	ONE PUTT	TWO PUTT	THREE PUTTS-Plus	EXPECTED PUTTS AVG.
1 foot	100%	0.0%	0.0%	1.001
2 feet	99%	0.6%	0.1%	1.009
3 feet	95%	5%	0.2%	1.053
4 feet	86%	14%	0.2%	1.147
5 feet	75%	25%	0.3%	1.256
6 feet	65%	35%	0.3%	1.357
7 feet	56%	44%	0.4%	1.443
7 feet, 10 inches	50%	49%	0.5%	1.50
8 feet	49%	51%	0.5%	1.515
9 feet	43%	56%	0.6%	1.575
10 feet	38%	61%	0.7%	1.626
11 feet	34%	65%	0.8%	1.669
12 feet	30%	69%	0.9%	1.705
13 feet	27%	72%	1%	1.737
14 feet	25%	74%	1%	1.765
15 feet	22%	77%	!%	1.790
16 feet	20%	78%	1%	1.811
17 feet	19%	80%	2%	1.830
18 feet	17%	81%	2%	1.848
19 feet	16%	83%	2%	1.863
20 feet	14%	84%	2%	1.878
21 feet	13%	85%	2%	1.891
22 feet	12%	85%	3%	1.903
23 feet	11%	86%	3%	1.914
24 feet	11%	86%	3%	1.924
25 feet	10%	87%	3%	1.934

Of course I would love to make every putt but that's not happening. What I really want is the least overall number of putts per round. And unfortunately chasing a one putt can lead to a three putt!

Based on the data above shorter than 8 feet the pros are closer to a 1 putt. So it would be fair to pick a pace and line within that distance to *'go for it'* more often.

But outside that distance the average is closer to a 2 putt so it would be sensible to pick a pace and line that would not 3 putt. That doesn't mean you are not trying to hole absolutely everything. You are just managing expectations and measuring yourself against what is normal from the relevant distance.

Next time you are over a long putt, be your own caddie, tell yourself, two putts from here and I am gaining shots on the field.

The psychological shift will mean you will put a better stroke on it and that will in turn help you to control your distance better.

d) My favourite putting tip is ... *Don't look up!*

Sounds simple I know, but trust me it works for a variety of reasons.
If you are anxious about a putt you might look up prematurely to check if it's gone in, this can cause problems controlling the putter face. I make a conscious effort to not look up for a couple of seconds after contacting the ball.
Sir Nick Faldo would focus on a blade of grass hidden by the ball until he would hear the ball drop into the cup.
Practice with this in mind and have this as your last thought next time you are feeling anxious over a putt.

Section 2: Developing your perfect routine

7. Quiet eye

The eyes focus on around 50 different things every second!

That is a lot of information going to your brain. Your brain has to interpret this information and then send instructions to your muscles to begin a motion. If your eyes are 'all over the place' it is hard to be precise when sending that information across. This is the essence of the theory behind the quiet eye.

A steadier final fixation, just before the critical moment, marks out the expert athletes, who hold their gaze for 62% longer than novices.
Expert athletes actually slowed down their thinking at the crucial moment.
The quiet eye allows you to soak in all the information from the object in question which helps you to produce the best motor response.
The quiet eye appears to help the brain plan the body's movements for a more fluid motion.

"Quiet eye" is described as an enhanced level of visual perception that allows the athlete to eliminate any distractions as they plan their next move

The initial research around the topic was done by Dr Joan Vickers at the University of Calgary(2004). She found that there was a difference between experts and beginners when putting. The better putters had a more stable last look at the ball before starting the putt. Beginners however had more erratic eye movements, i.e with less specific focus and concentration.

Further to this, Dr Samuel Vine of Exeter university found that elite golfers continue to fixate on the spot where the golf ball was after they hit it.
Elite putters also trace the intended path of the putt with their eyes more accurately prior to putting.

Control of eye movements can vary between players depending on the quality of eye muscle control. This eye muscle control can be trained with specific exercises. If you find your putting performance varies and deteriorates toward the end of a round/multiple rounds then this may be due to eye muscle fatigue.

"There is a small window of opportunity for the motor system to receive information from the eyes," explains Sam Vine at the University of Exeter. "And experts have found a better way to optimise that window and to keep that window [open], which helps their movements to be really accurate and really precise."

An effective quiet eye period consists of:
(1) a single, long, continuous fixation on the back of the ball;
(2) an onset before backswing; i.e a trigger

(3) a continued fixation through the backstroke, forestroke and contact (i.e do not look up)
(4) a dwell time after contact ie still looking down after you make contact

This period of focus is especially important for pressure putts. The quiet eye act of steadying yourself is how you get into a state of **'flow' or 'being in the zone'** – At this point the concentration feels effortless, where you are thinking of nothing else. The quiet eye period also seems to coincide with other changes throughout the body. The **heart rate temporarily decelerates** and the movement of the limbs becomes smoother.

Examples of athletes that used quiet eye:

Steph Curry (NBA) - phenomenal accuracy when shooting the basketball, at varying distances and in clutch moments.
Serena Williams (tennis) - intense focus and playing one point at a time was always very important for Serena.
Christiano Ronaldo (football) - note how he steadies his breathing before a penalty and focuses with intensity on the football. For free kicks he used to line up the valve and aim to hit that exact spot on the ball.
Johnny Wilkinson (Rugby union) - had phenomenal success in kicking points/conversions. If you watch his pre-kick routine it was very consistent, measured and deliberate. He always focused on a far point (a lady in the crowd, a few rows up). He tracked his eyes from the ball to the distant target in the crowd, slowly and deliberately, he controlled his breathing, he committed and

executed with game changing results. He raised the standard with his results and now most kickers have replicated this **pre-kick routine.**

8. The importance of a pre-putt routine

If you don't have a routine your mind can wander, doubt can creep in. You may start to have thoughts which are unproductive, you will be inconsistent in your stroke. If you have a set routine which takes the same time every time you will have a checklist of thoughts to tick off which will ultimately end in a committed stroke and better results.

"Technically Good = Mentally Good"

Dan Grieve - from his excellent book on chipping technique 'The 3 Releases'

Developing good technique gives you so much more 'insurance' over a putt. Even if you misjudge it a little or mishit it a little, it will still give you a satisfactory result and avoid a terrible putt. Simply knowing you are correctly set-up to a putt with a good plan in mind gives you confidence to execute.

<u>Recommended pre putt routine:</u>

There are two stages:
    1) The thinking/planning stage
    2) The execution stage

It's important to separate the two. Once you start your execution stage, you must have minimum thoughts, ideally zero thoughts. This is where you need to have bulletproof focus.

1) Planning
-Is it uphill or downhill?
-Left or right breaking (or both)?
-Read the putt from at least two viewpoints (behind the hole and front on), but ideally from four viewpoints.
-Gauge the distance to the hole by tracing the putt
-Trace the path from ball to hole
-Slowly and smoothly trace the path the ball will take with the break/slope now factored in
-Establish an aim point or a ghost hole that you will build your stance aligned towards
-Line your ball up pointing along the line you want to start, i.e aiming at the intermediate target/ghost hole

2) Executing
-Look at the hole and then directly at the ghost hole, look at a small point on the ball
-Try and keep your eye movements smooth and deliberate at this point
-Initiate your trigger movement (eg. forward press the putter slightly) and putt

-Keep looking at the spot where the ball was
-Pick the ball out of the cup

9. How to get in the zone (and stay in it)

What's really important in being in the zone is controlling which sense is in charge.
When we are playing golf we do use other senses eg. listening for the wind.
But during a shot we want to block out all other senses and just be using the visual system.

Earl Woods would help Tiger practise shutting out the outside noise by trying to distract him mid shot. This undoubtedly helped Tiger to play better than his peers especially when faced with large crowds.

Tiger recently said he is always trying to distract Charlie (i.e it's part of his training)
Tiger told Charlie; I want you to be so focused on your next shot that you forget to breathe.

Concentrating with intense focus can be learned/practised.

Getting in the zone is about:
-Intense focus and concentration
-Using quiet eye techniques (see above)
-Sticking to your pre putt routine
(This means the process becomes automatic/muscle memory takes over)

-Forming a clear mental picture of what is about to happen (visualisation)
-Not having thoughts once you initiate the putt (mental chatter occupies your bodies resources and hinders performance)

10.Visualise your putt with a tracer.

During TV coverage a tool often used on screen is an ideal line for the ball to travel to the hole (sometimes with a max and min break and everything in between). You should do this in your mind too. By tracing from the ball to the hole, see a full line. This will also help you with speed control as you will associate the time it takes for your eyes to travel along the trace with how long the putt will take to travel to the hole.

Smooth eye movements and good peripheral vision help when using your eyes to trace the path of the putt.

We don't want our eye muscles to be jerky when doing this, i.e being smooth is the goal.

If you are questioning the line, ask yourself, If I hit a straight putt from here, where will it miss? If the answer is left, ask yourself, by how much? Then adjust accordingly. You're asking yourself questions that have simple, affirmative answers, and you'll be in a more positive frame of mind.

"Watch your thoughts, they become your words;

watch your words, they become your actions;

watch your actions, they become your habits;

watch your habits, they become your character;

watch your character, it becomes your destiny."

LAO TZU

Section 3 : Eye Exercises

11. Eye alignment and distance control tendencies

If your eyes pull out (exophoria) generally you will miss long. This is generally for patients who are short sighted.
If your eyes pull in (esophoria) generally you will miss short. This is generally for patients who are long sighted.
If your eyes have straight alignment you are in luck! (orthophoria)

To check for this see your optometrist but you can try this self test too:

Look at a (distant) target
Cover one eye with your hand
Cover each eye in turn (alternate the cover between eyes a few times)

If the target moves with your hand (i.e same direction) then you have an exo tendency
Exos judge things further away than esos
Exos tend to miss long more often

If the target moves against your hand (i.e in the opposite direction you are moving your hand) then you have an eso tendency
Esos tend to miss short.

If the target does not move as you move your hand then you have straight alignment (orthophoria)

Now repeat this test with a closer target

Some people have different muscle alignment depending on how close the target is.
This could mean a different tendency for short putts and a different tendency for long putts.

If your putting performance declines as you get tired your eye alignment control may be changing with fatigue.

Eye exercises aim to move you to generally straighter alignment and more consistent alignment over distances and time.
Even when we are aligned normally we can still train for endurance.

12. The Bug Walk (for smooth eye movements)

This exercise is to improve your eye tracking to make your tracing smooth when visualising a putt.

This is particularly helpful if you find it difficult to read putts when you play a multi round event, or towards the end of a round your eyes frequently get tired when lining up putts.

Attach a string to a doorknob.
Hold the string up to your nose, as golfers, this exercise should be done with the string pointing down from our nose to the door knob (as we look down to the green). So do this exercise standing up.

The single string will appear double but the images will cross where your eyes are pointing
Imagine there is a bug walking from your nose end to the doorknob end
Initially you will see the string(s) as a V
Then as you get further down it will appear as an X
Trace your eyes up and down the string 5 times

When you first start the tracing may be unsmooth and feel like your eyes are not aiming/pointing exactly where you want them to. As you repeat the exercise your eye movement control should become more accurate and smoother.

To push yourself further you can add 3 beads to the string.

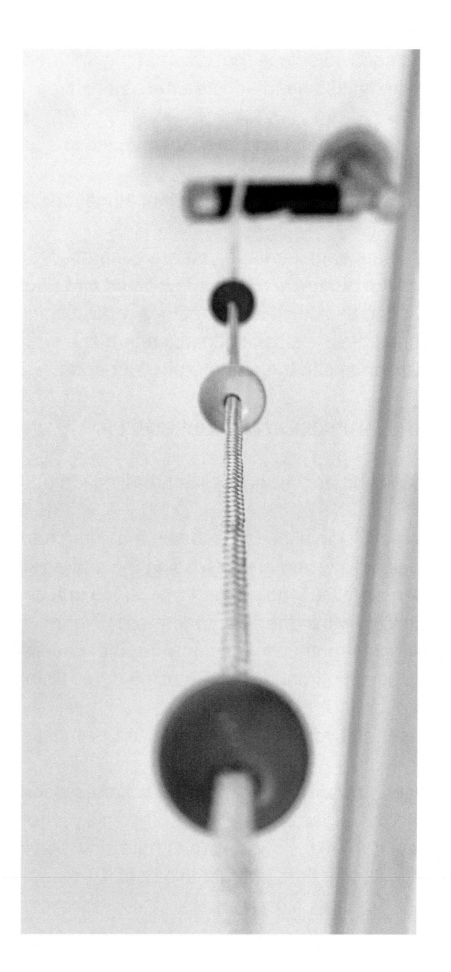

The goal is to see two strings that cross at the first bead.
Next look at the middle bead and see the strings cross at that bead.
Now look at the third bead and see the strings cross at that final bead.
Jump between the beads maintaining that string crossing.

If one string disappears it means you are suppressing one eye and favouring the other eye. Blink a few times and attempt to refocus and bring back the X. Sometimes repositioning the string slightly will bring the eyes back into alignment and you will see the X again but try and keep the string up to your nose.

13. Peripheral awareness for green reading.

This is helpful if you are struggling with reading lag putts.

Good peripheral vision allows you to see a bigger picture. If you look at a green initially you are assessing the overall slope of the green. So generally the whole green may slope in a certain direction and then within the green there are different smaller slopes. So for short putts you may only need to understand the break as you see it in front of you, i.e using direct vision or central vision.
But for a longer putt you need to see the line overall combining various mini-reads.
Better peripheral awareness results in quicker assessment of the total read of a putt. I see some players rush this part of the game and although I don't like slow play (ok I hate slow play!) I think it's important to take your time and get this right. Remember to start

reading your putt as you approach the green and also when your playing partners are preparing to putt.

Rush to your ball, but not over your ball.

To improve your peripheral awareness I recommend the use of a peripheral expansion chart.

1. Stick the chart on the wall at eye level
2. With one eye covered look directly at the central letter/target
3. Don't look around but be aware of the surrounding letters using your peripheral vision
4. How far out can you read the letters using your peripheral vision?
5. Repeat with the other eye
6. Repeat with both eyes open

To make the test more difficult, re-print the expansion chart as a larger version.

The closer you stand to the chart the harder it will be, if the central target is blurred you are too close.

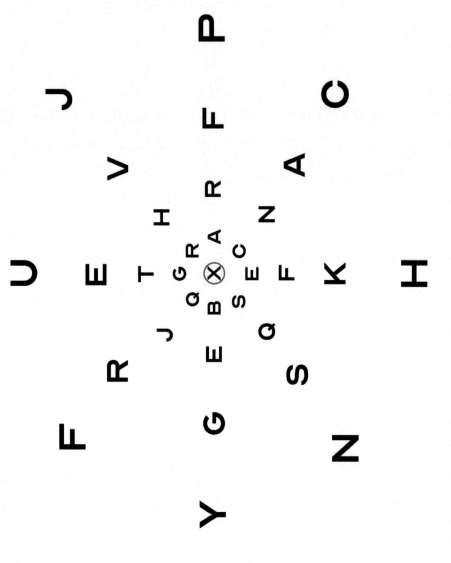

Section 4: Strategy/How to aim

14.What is the apex?

When the ball travels along the ideal path to the hole, it passes a high point. This is the apex of the putt.
If the putt travels inside the apex line the putt will miss low
If the putt travels outside the apex line it will miss high
However this next bit is really important
You shouldn't aim for the apex
You should aim for a point on the green which (with the correct pace) will allow the ball to pass the apex point and go in the hole. This is a point above the apex. (Better putters aim higher!)
You should read this and visualise this for every putt and then putt to an imaginary point. The imaginary point is your aim point/ghost hole.
Then when you putt you are putting straight to the aim point but gravity will take care of the curve. **Every Putt is a Straight Putt**

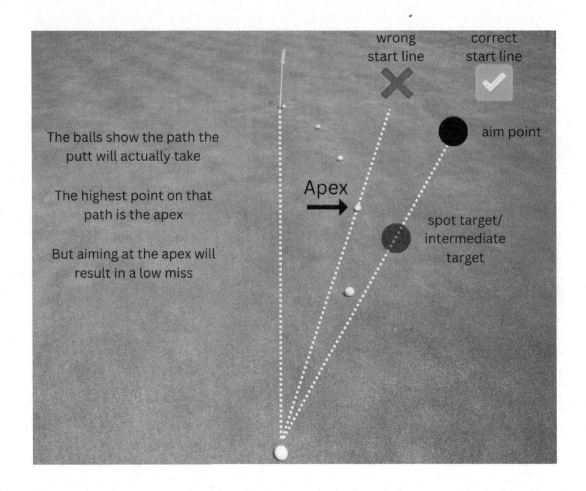

The balls show the path the putt will actually take

The highest point on that path is the apex

But aiming at the apex will result in a low miss

15 What is the high side?

When we read a putt we assess the slope of a green. eg. left to right. The high side is the side of the hole that is physically higher. In this example the left side.

When aiming a putt we want to give it the maximum chance of dropping in the hole. If we miss on the low side the ball cannot drop in. If a putt is lacking pace it will miss on the low side, which is frustrating. However if we miss on the high side and the weight is correct gravity drops the ball in. *(If you smash the putt the high side is irrelevant)*

When facing a long putt aiming for the high side is likely to leave you a shorter second putt because if you miss the ball will be feeding back into the hole.
If you miss low, the ball will continue to travel away from the hole leaving you a longer second putt.

If we are slightly on the low side with perfect pace it will miss
If we are slightly on the high side it might be missing but if its deadweight it has a second chance to go in (gravity)

Dave Pelz, one of the world's leading short game gurus, conducted a study on putting.
The study took place over years and involved thousands of putts. He compiled data from every type of player- tour pros and the average golfer. The study showed that regardless of skill level, most golfers under-read putts.

The facts revealed that of all putts missed, 85% miss on the low side of the hole. The study also revealed that golfers who more regularly miss on the high side of the hole make more putts.

Players who regularly miss on the low side 3-putt much more often because on average the ball finishes farther from the hole.

So *aiming for the high side if we are in doubt is optimal as it will mean more 1 putts but also less 3 putts*. The high side is also known as the pro-side.

Aim for the Pro side

High side   Low

AimPurePuttPure

16.Why do downhill putts break more?

How much a putt breaks is inherently linked to the pace the ball is travelling. For an uphill putt the ball needs to be hit harder to get to the hole. For the first part of the putt the ball will be travelling too fast to be affected by the break. Near the hole the ball will slow down relatively and "take the break". So for uphill putts focus your read on what happens close to the hole.

For downhill putts the ball needs to be stroked with a more gentle pace, unless you want a long putt coming back! So for the whole length of the putt it will be travelling slower. If it's travelling slower it will take all the break for the whole putt. In fact for some downhill putts the ball gathers momentum and pace and gets faster towards the end. So for downhill putts the break at the beginning is particularly important.

The first part of reading a putt is establishing if it's uphill or downhill! Pace is key. Everything else follows from this.

17. The hole gets smaller the faster you hit your putt !

Pace is as important (if not more important!) than the line.

If you deadweight putts and play for more break you will be a more consistent putter. Good days will be lots of putts dropping. Bad days will be not so many dropping but proximity to the hole for your return putt will be close and as a result you will have less three putts and you will not lose momentum due to lack of confidence on the greens.

If you take less break and ram the putts, good days will be good with putts dropping, but bad days you will have some nasty lip outs and you may lose confidence and momentum on the day.

Putting is not about forcing them in, it's about playing the percentages over the course of a round/week/month/season.

For a "free putt" in a Matchplay situation, the adjustment to pace and line is very small. There is no point ramming the putt and not allowing it to take the break. And, we don't want to make the hole smaller.

You may have heard the phrase "never up, never in" and although this is true the reality is hitting a putt too hard actually makes the hole smaller.

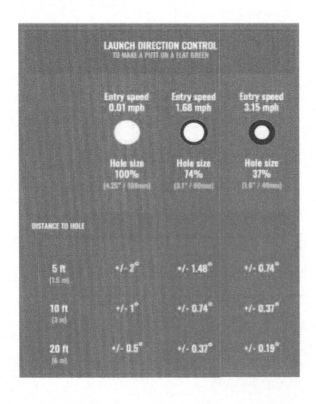

Trackman data (April 2020) which demonstrates that the hole gets smaller the faster you hit your putts

18. Distance control

For consistent distance control you need #tempo and reducing variables. Sounds simple, because it is !

- Hit the middle of the putter face every time
- Don't flip your wrist
- Don't grip tighter
- Don't sway your body
- Control the length of your putts by adjusting the length of your backswing

Distance control is something that needs to be practised a lot. As green speed varies daily (grass length, temperature, rainfall the day before etc etc) we need to dial in green speed on the day for accurate distance control.

Section 5 Drills for Skills

19. Putting Drills

Find your weakness and turn it into your strength!

We need to be honest with ourselves in analysing what to spend more time on. If we divide putting into sections:

19a Distance control (lag putts)
19b Tempo/transition/stroke
19c Start line
19d Holing 'makeable' putts
19e Green reading and visualisation
19f Pre round suggested warm up routine

Does your handicap overall match your level in these individual sections?

Overall it will cancel out

Now you need to focus practice on the weak areas. It would be easy to repeat what we are good at, building confidence etc but that's not how we progress.

We need to feel uncomfortable to improve.

Read that last bit again.

19a. Putting drills for distance control

Distance control drill 1: The ladder drill

Do this drill initially on a flat surface, but later do it on an uphill and downhill putt too.

You start with a putt that needs to land within a zone which you have marked out.

If you are successful distance wise and it finishes between the two markers, you go further back and try again. Keep going until you don't get it within your goal distance.

If you miss, start again.

How large your goal zone is depends on how good you are but the smaller your zone the harder the drill will be and the better you will get with your distance control.

You can mark your goal zone with tees, ball markers or flat ghost holes. I suggest keeping them a foot apart initially but work towards a 6 inch target.

Distance control drill 2.

If you have tendency to leave putts short or long you can modify this drill either way to penalise your tendency

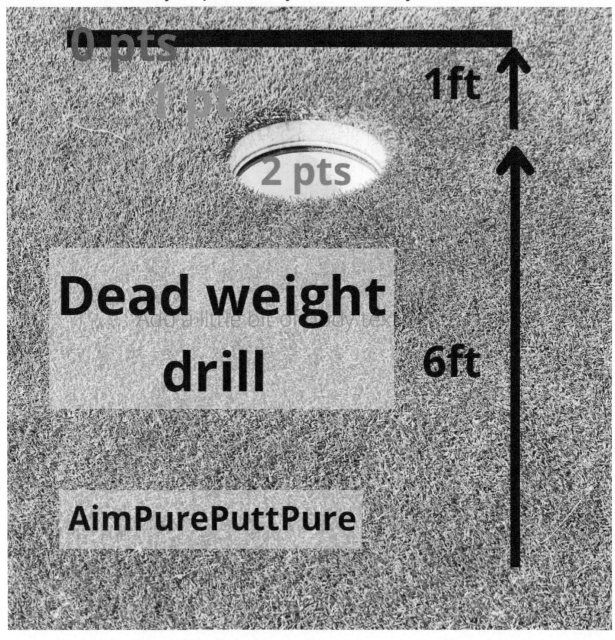

If you tend to putt past the hole, putt to a hole with an alignment stick behind it as a backstop
(1 foot behind the hole for 6 feet putts, 2 feet behind the hole for 12 feet putts)

If you hole the putt - 2 points
If you miss but you are not past the alignment stick - 1 point
If you hit the stick - 0 points

10 putts from both distances

What's your score?

Record the score so next time you know if you are improving

If your tendency is to leave putts short use an alignment stick level with a point you must get past
If you hole the putt 2 points
If you miss but get past the alignment stick 1 point
If you are short of the alignment stick 0 points

This is also a good warm up drill to get the pace

Distance tip 1 when practising: look at the hole whilst putting
i.e keep your head up the whole time, this will help you keep the target and distance in mind the whole time instead of focussing on the ball and the mechanics of the stroke.

Distance tip 2 when practising: use a towel with markings on it at set intervals

Use the marks to gauge how far back and through you bring the putter. Control the distance by length of stroke is more consistent than trying to 'hit it harder'

Distance tip 3 when playing: look at the hole for 5 seconds before pulling the trigger but then look at the ball for your stroke. This will keep the target and distance in mind but allow you to make a clean stroke.

19b. Tempo/transition drill

Try this to improve the tempo of your stroke and the transition.

Keep a coin on the back of your putter.

The aim is to keep the penny on the putter for as long as possible.

If your tempo/transition is jerky the coin will fall off.

Think smooooth.

If the putts don't go in at the beginning with this drill don't worry, but notice how your pace control gets better when the coin stays on.

Using a metronome for tempo

Download an app on your smartphone that has a metronome feature. When putting the ideal tempo should be between 75 and 80 beats per minute.

Have the metronome set at this rhythm and putt to the same rhythm.

Again this will lead to a more consistent stroke.

Controlling the putter face

You should set your stance up around the putter face aiming where you want the ball to start. But if during the stroke the putter face opens or closes at the moment of impact you are not going to aim where you want it to go. A common theme amongst good putters is consistent putter face control. The wrists should be quiet when putting and this helps stabilise the putter face. Rocking the shoulders using a pendulum action is more consistent and ideal.

To check and improve this, adopt a putting stance and place an alignment stick between your sternum and the top of your putter head. With deliberate steady practice strokes the rod and putter should be moving together i.e no separation. If your wrists get involved the alignment stick will separate from your putter.

Alignment stick and putter are connected (less wrist involvement)

Alignment stick and putter are disconnected due to wrist involvement.

19c. Start line

The coin drill for start line

For this drill, set up a straight putt and place a coin or small object on the green as a target. Try to hit the coin with your putt, and repeat the drill several times to improve your aim. By making the target smaller you will tighten up your start line and it will give you a lot of confidence when putting to a standard size hole.

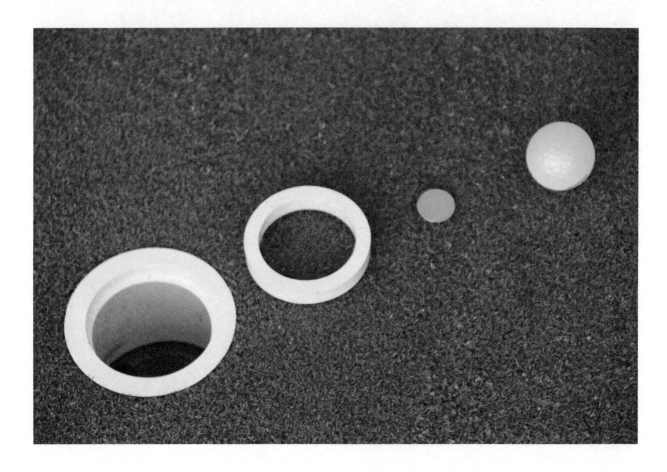

Cup reducers are available, to convert the hole into a small/extra small hole, but putting to a small coin or ball marker works well too.

The goalkeeper drill for high side

Using some tees block the low side of the hole (remember to tap down once you remove the tees)

This makes the hole smaller and so you will have to focus on hitting your start line even more

Make some putts with the ball entering on the high side.

The hole is big enough! And this will get you used to seeing the ball enter from the high side.

It will also help you dial in the correct pace to not smash it through the break. No nasty lip outs please.

If you are going to miss, miss high (but don't miss)

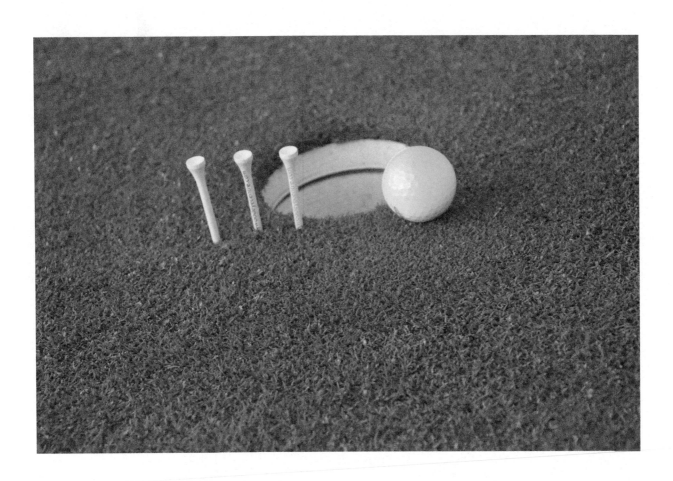

19c and d.

How to use an elevated string line
This will help with start line and stroke.
Essentially two knitting needles and a string to putt underneath.
The beginning and end needles should be 8-10 feet apart.
Put one needle in where you want to start from and one in directly
behind the centre of the hole.

Set up square to the hole position with a ball under the line (half of the ball either side of the string)
Looking down at the ball you should be directly above the ball.
You can now look along the line of the path.

(ideal)

(too far over the string)

(too far behind the string)

Assuming it's a flat putt with no break, if you putt straight back and straight through using the string as a guide for your stroke the ball would go in the middle.
If there is some break the putt will miss accordingly to the relevant side.

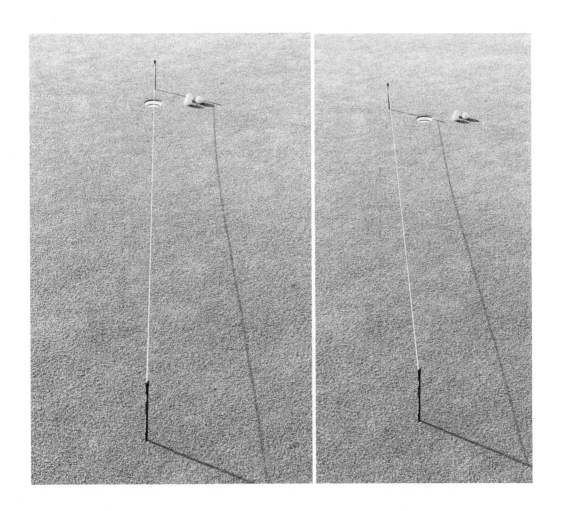

To adjust for break you move the needle behind the hole to the opposite side that the initial batch of balls ended on.
Ie if the balls ended 2 cups to the right we move the string 2 cups to the left.
More breaks would need more compensation.
Again when putting now to the straight compensated target i.e. your aim point, the balls should go in.

This will give you feedback on a variety of things
-your stroke
-are you hitting the start line
-pace - if your line is correct but you are putting it through the break (lip outs or missing high and finishing too far behind the hole)

-how much you need to correct for slope and general green reading feedback

It will also help you understand the margin for error to still make a putt at various speeds. Decreasing the pace of your putts to deadweight increases the margin for error on line!

19e. Green reading and Visualization drill

This is about having a putt planned out in your mind, not just the line but the pace and the line, everything.

You will need a friend with a timer.

Do a pretend putt without a ball first, but map it out in your head and get your friend to time it, i.e how long you think it will take to reach the hole. Hit the imaginary ball and say out loud: ok its started, its halfway, its taking the break now more, it's near the hole, it's in.
Note how long the pretend putt took to 'go in'
Then repeat it with a ball. Get your friend to time it again.
How far out were you? If you have a tendency to leave lag putts short, are you visualising the putts as being faster on the clock than they actually are/should be?

19f. Pre round putting warm up

Start with short putts. See the ball drop in a lot. This will help with confidence. Short putts also help with getting the start line correct. On the course you are expected to make short putts so it's important to be rock solid with them.

Usually I make a circle around the hole (putting with different breaks is important too)

Keep completing the circle until I don't miss any, then make the circle bigger.

Then alternate short and long putts but still going around in a circle.

Next choose one of the distance control drills described above.

Finish with one ball to varying holes on the practice green, but go through your routine like you would on the course.

For this last bit in particular try and hole every putt, replicate your intensity of focus that you want to have on the course

Stick to your pre putt routine, read it, line it up, step in, execute.

Be conscious of the quiet eye technique at this stage.

'Discipline is doing what you hate to do but doing it like you love it'
Mike Tyson

Practice practice practice, until it becomes automatic

Section 6 Miscellaneous

20. Which sunglasses are best for golfers?

Can I just wear a hat?

Which tint colour is best?

A hat only stops the light coming in from one angle and we need to be mindful of the light bouncing off the ground (which can cause distracting glare).

Luke Donald is a good example of a hat wearer, the crows feet near his eyes probably would have been prevented with sunglasses.

Justin Rose wears sunglasses not only to protect from UV light but also to keep pollen out as he suffers from allergies.

Golfers spend a lot of time outdoors and over a lifetime the extra light exposure can speed up ageing of the eyes (cataracts and macula degeneration)

Sunglasses with UV protection are a must for golfers.

The bulk of the time we are on the course we are in between shots, that's when the sunnies need to be protecting your eyes.

- Darker tints do not necessarily offer more protection
- Polarising sunglasses reduce glare and if possible always choose this

So depending on the light conditions you are playing in ideally you would have two pairs of sunglasses for golf:
- Grey is good for harsh/strong sun or very bright days, it's the darkest of the tints
- Brown/rose tints are best for contrast enhancing (green reading) and they are not as dark so you don't lose detail (again better for green reading). These lenses work best for moderate to high sun levels.
- Amber/yellow contrast lenses are good to "brighten up" a dull day. Cyclists often wear this lens colour so they can see the potholes better/earlier on a cloudy day.
- Some golfers particularly those with a prescription choose to wear lenses that react to the level of light/uv (transitions)

Speak to your local optician for expert advice, fitting and aftercare of your sunglasses.

<u>Glossary of terms</u>

Suppression: a subconscious adaptation by a person's brain to eliminate the symptoms of disorders of binocular vision i.e. the act of ignoring one eye, because a single image is better than a blurred/double image.

Lazy eye: deep/permanent suppression of an eye which is very difficult to improve after the age of 8

Dominant eye: is when you use one eye more than the other, have better vision in one eye, or can fixate on something better with one eye

Parallax: refers to the change in the apparent position of an object when viewed from different points

Intermediate/spot target: a point between our starting position and the hole that we line up towards

Aim point: if we draw a line extending from the intermediate/spot target this is known as the aim point (also known as the fake hole target)

"Quiet eye": is described as an enhanced level of visual perception that allows the athlete to eliminate any distractions as they plan their next move

<u>Summary</u>

Now what?

You should now have a good understanding of how and why you can be an amazing putter.

You have the knowledge and the routines to self diagnose and practice accordingly.

I recommend periodically referring back to the book, to make sure you are sticking to the principles outlined.

I also believe that having a professional look at your setup is a good idea. Even if this just gives you the confidence to commit.

Contact my office to arrange a personalised assessment; chorleywoodeyecentre.com

And remember,

<u>putt with commitment</u>

Thank you to all my friends and family for helping me in 'putting' this book together.

Thank you to Mariam Walji, photography/edits.

I would also like to thank Duncan Woolger PGA professional for helping me in editing this book and Moor Park Golf Club, Hertfordshire for images taken on location.

Printed in Great Britain
by Amazon

30479077R10044